NORTH AMERICAN ANIMALS

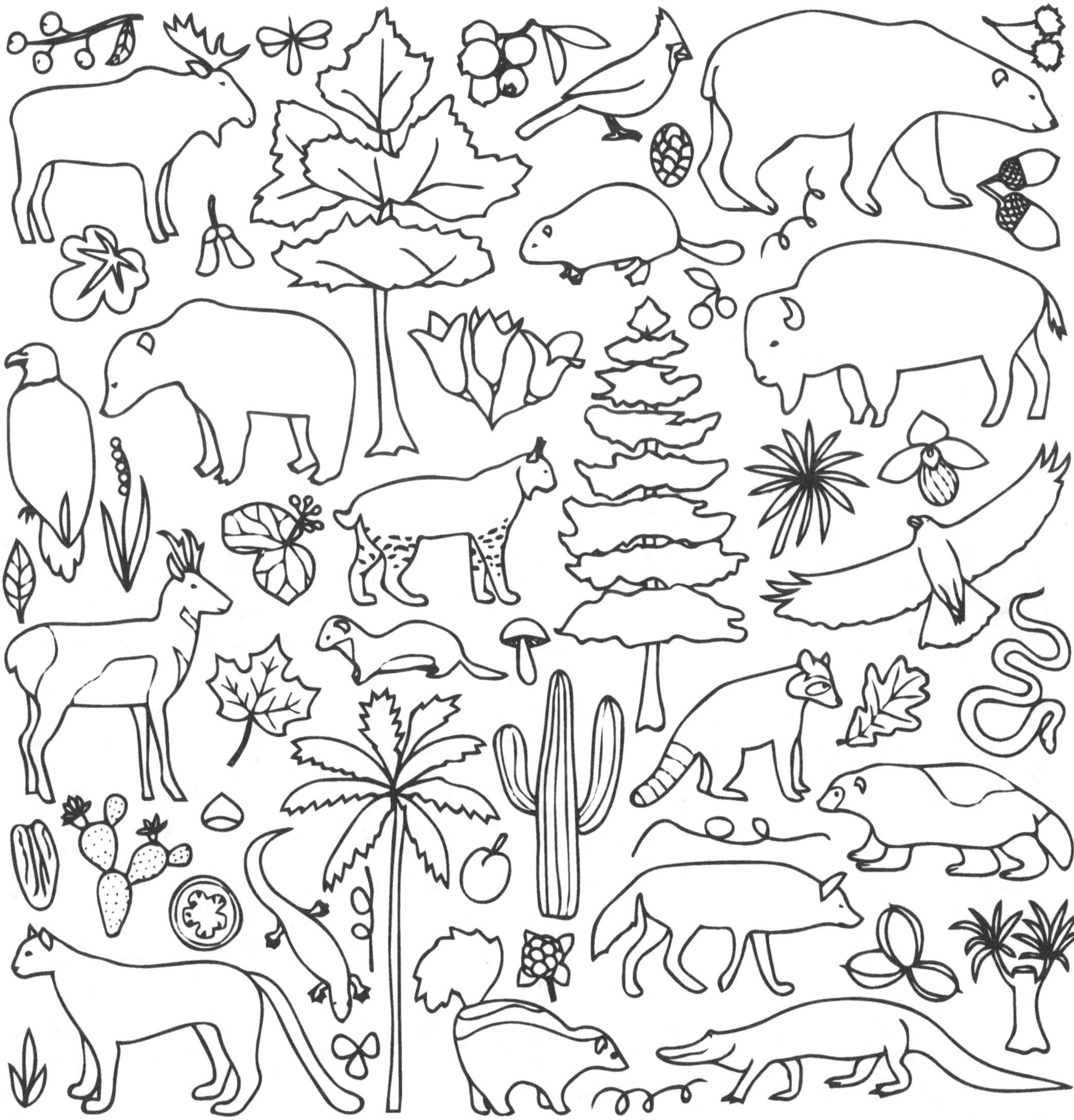

Titi's Book

Welcome to Titi Flower Design
Here you will have a pleasant experience if you are stressed.
We always create books to help you heal from within.
Help you overcome all your worries,
stress and love yourself.
Moreover, a good book can be a meaningful gift
for relatives, friends, and lovers.
TiTi's Book will always be with you.
Hope you will have a good experience
when shopping at Titi Flower Design.

Thanks a million!

Titi's Book

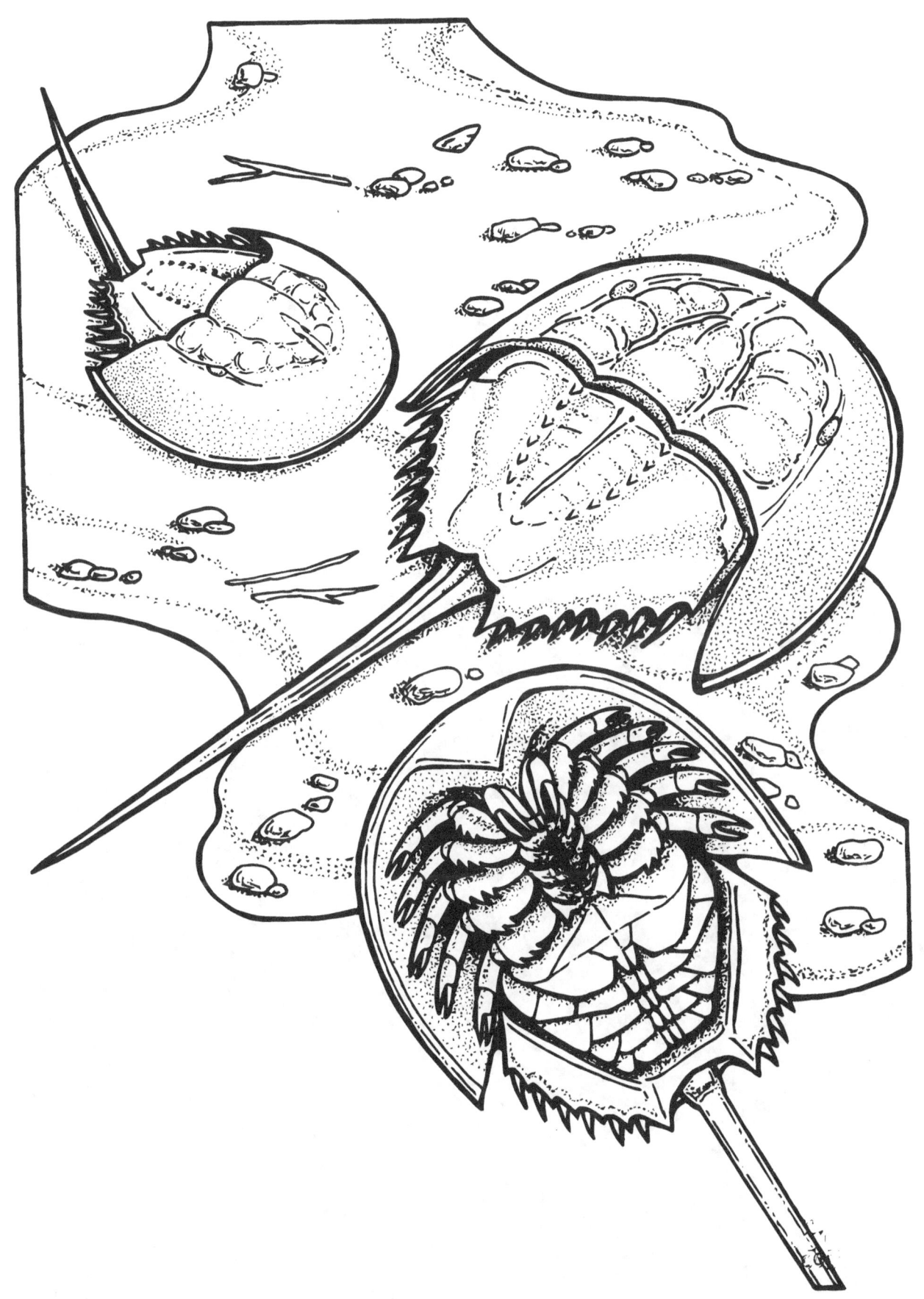

ATLANTIC HORSESHOE CRAB

Titis Book

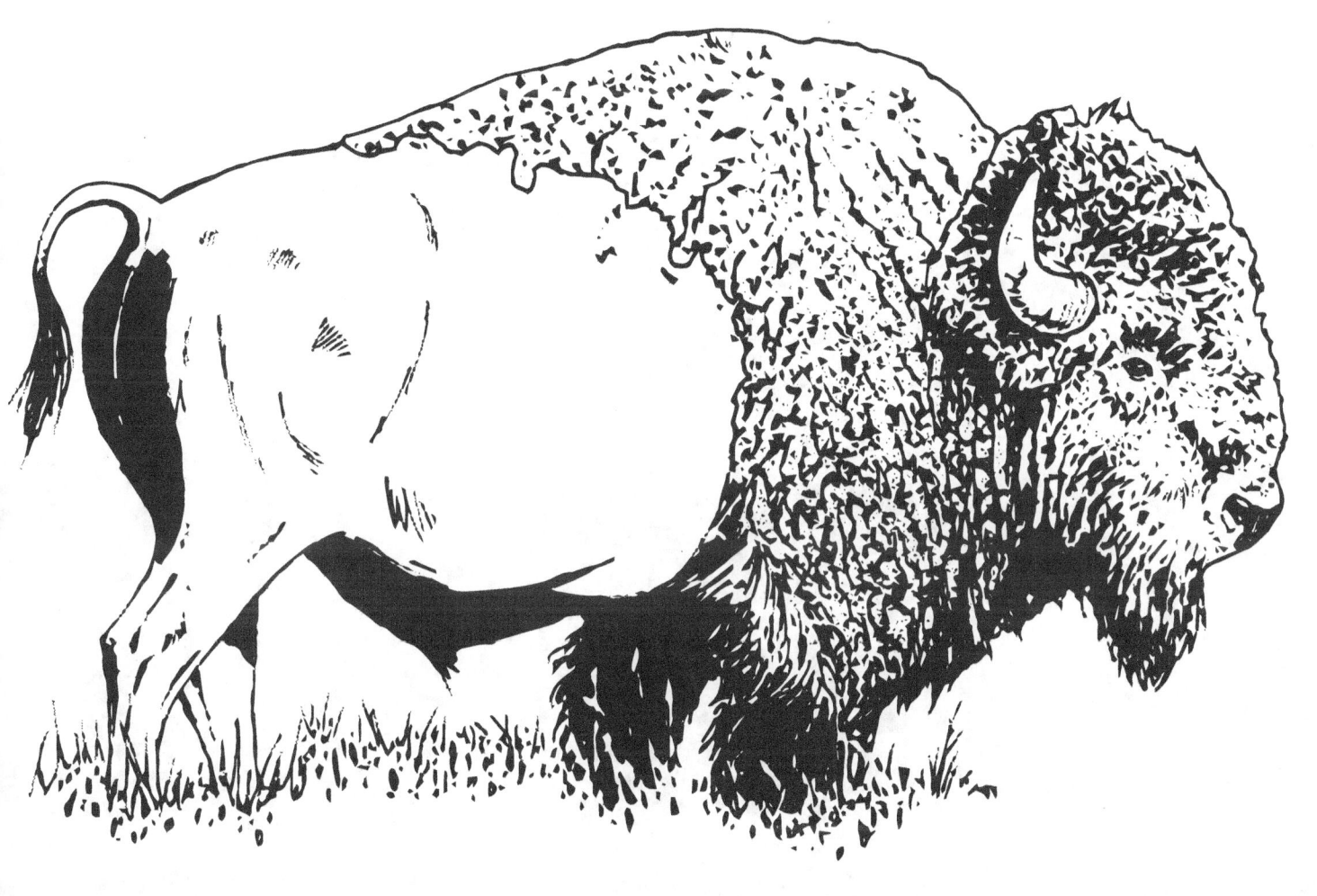

AMERICAN BISON

Titi's Book

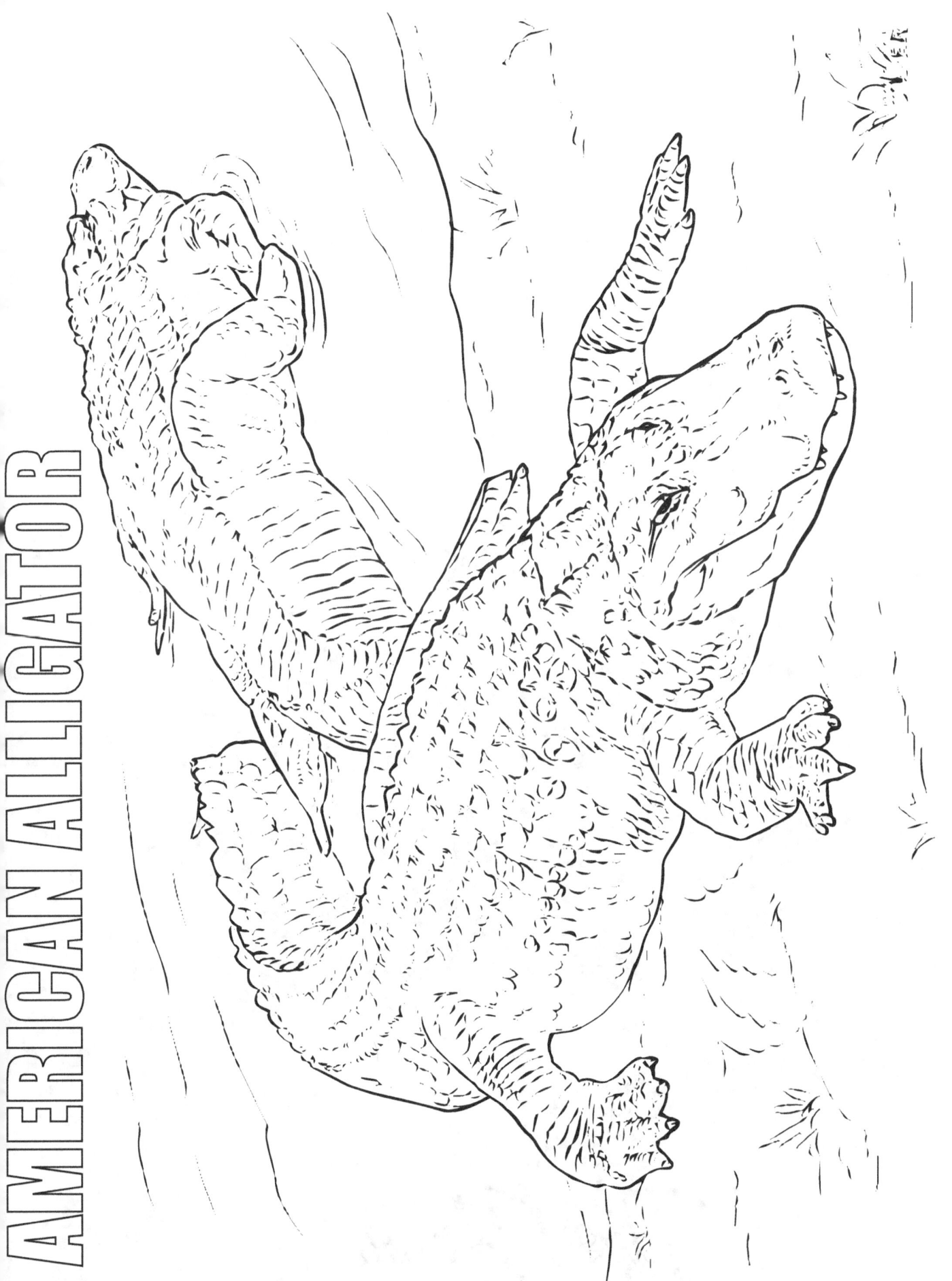

AMERICAN ALLIGATOR

Titi's Book

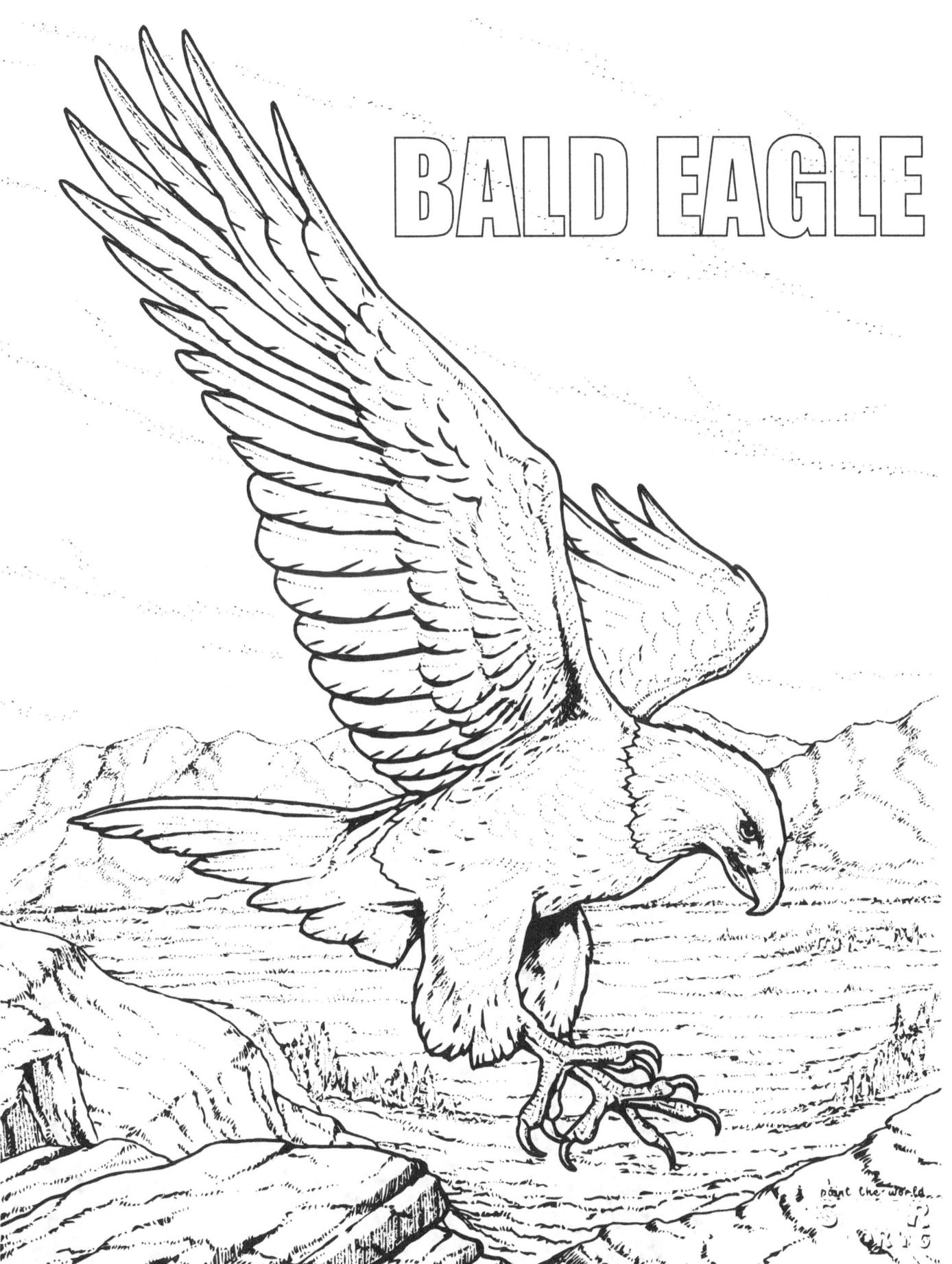

BALD EAGLE

Titi's Book

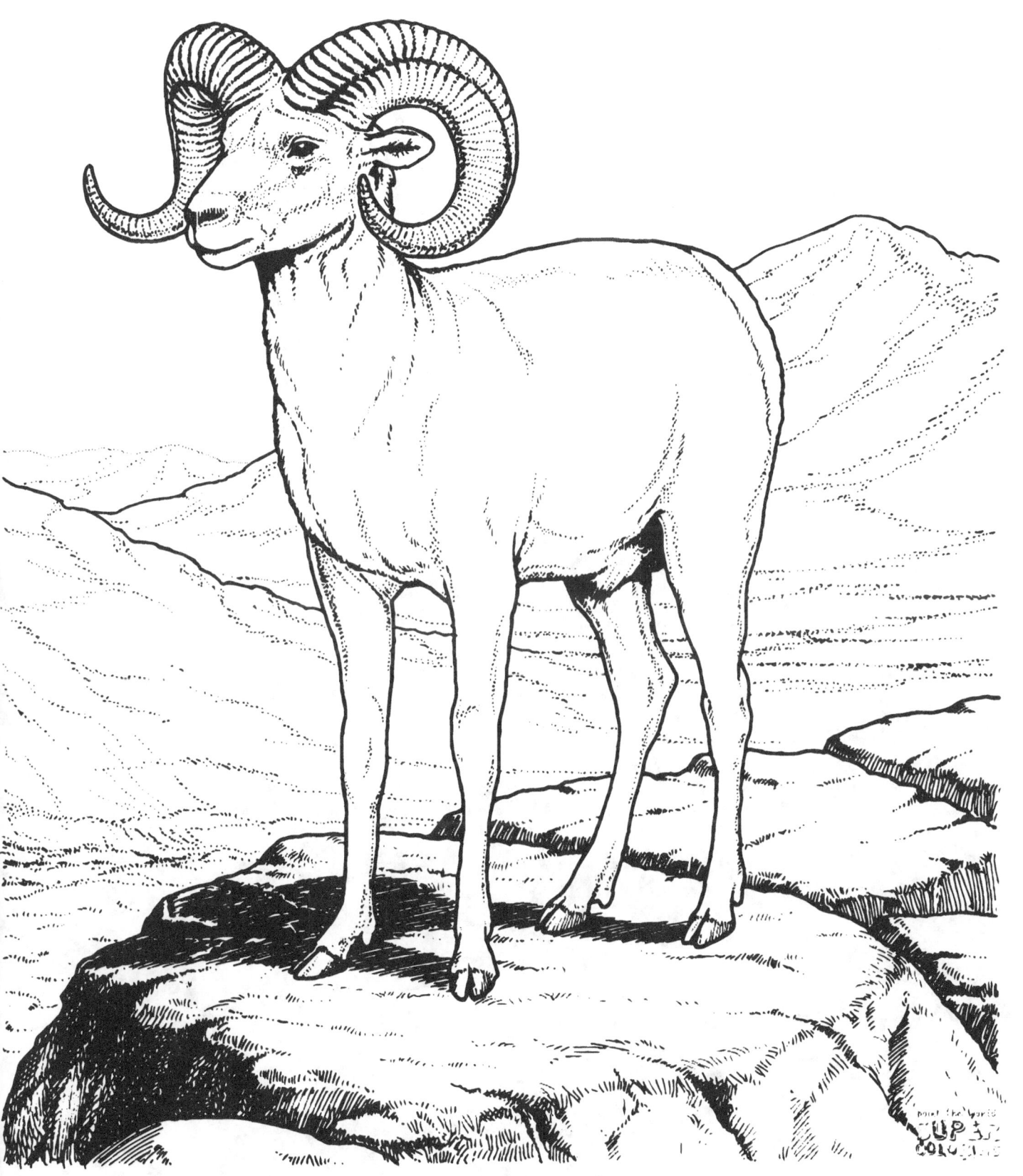

BIGHORN SHEEP

Titi's Book

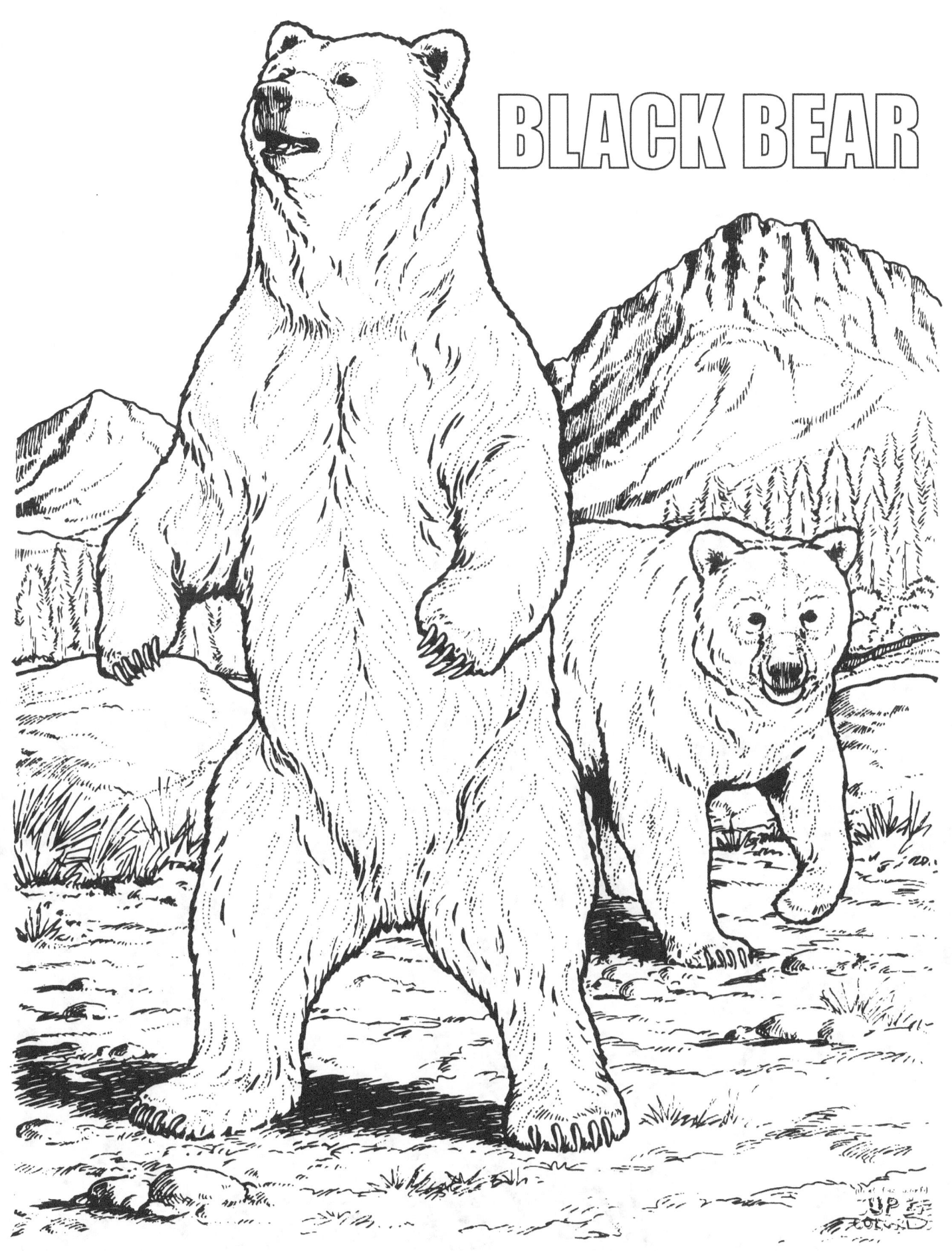

BLACK BEAR

Titis Book

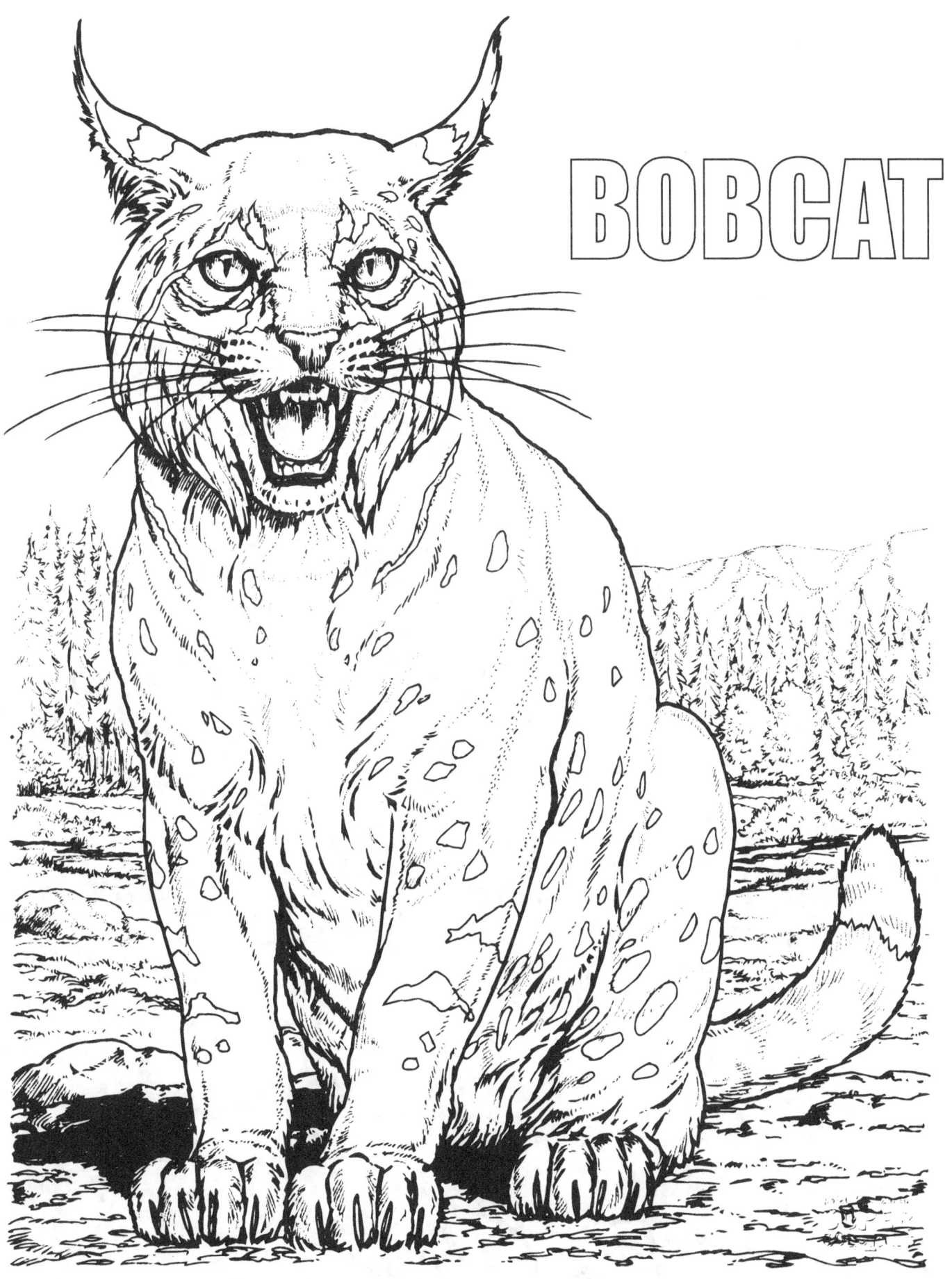

BOBCAT

Titi's Book

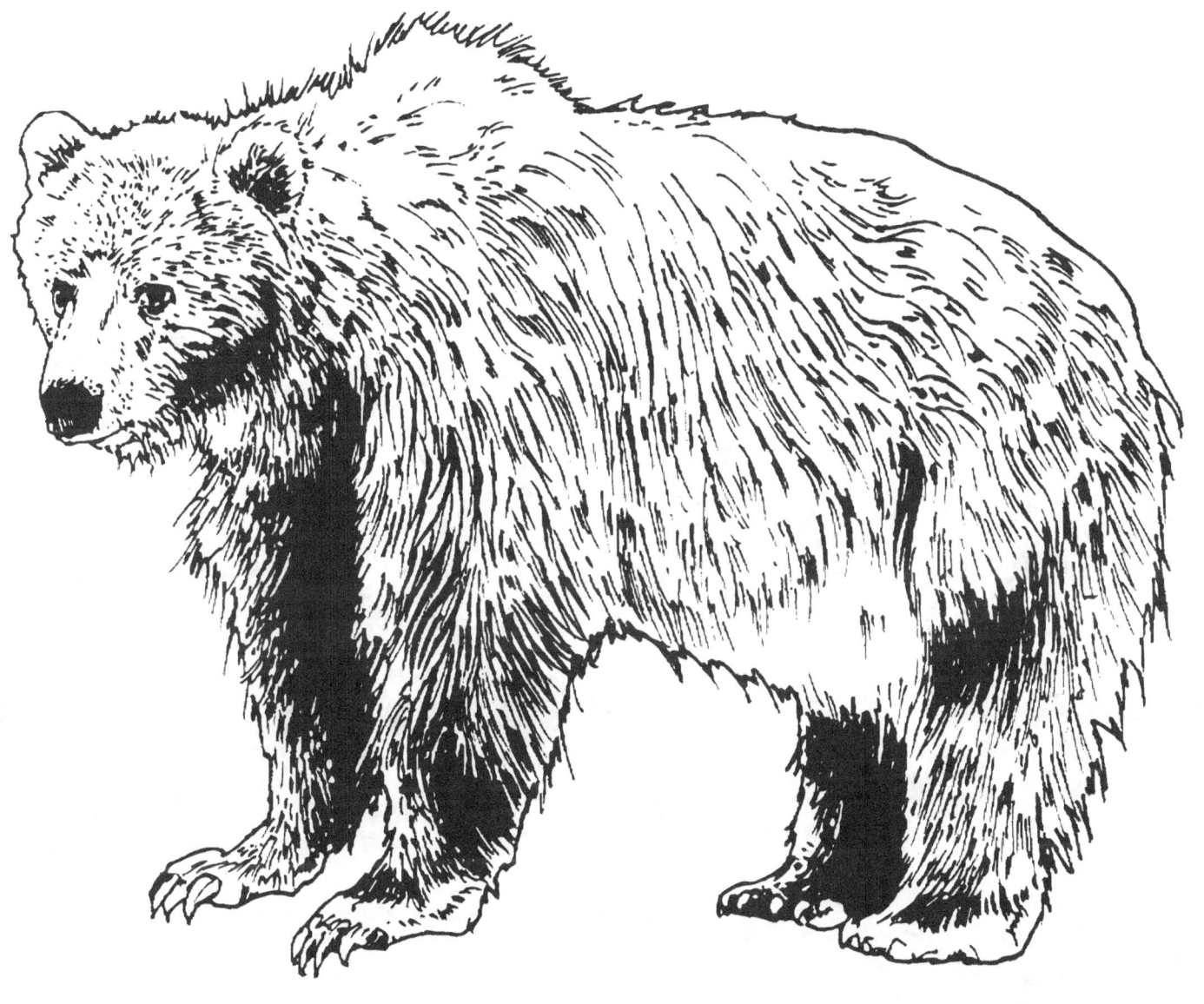

BROWN BEAR

Titis Book

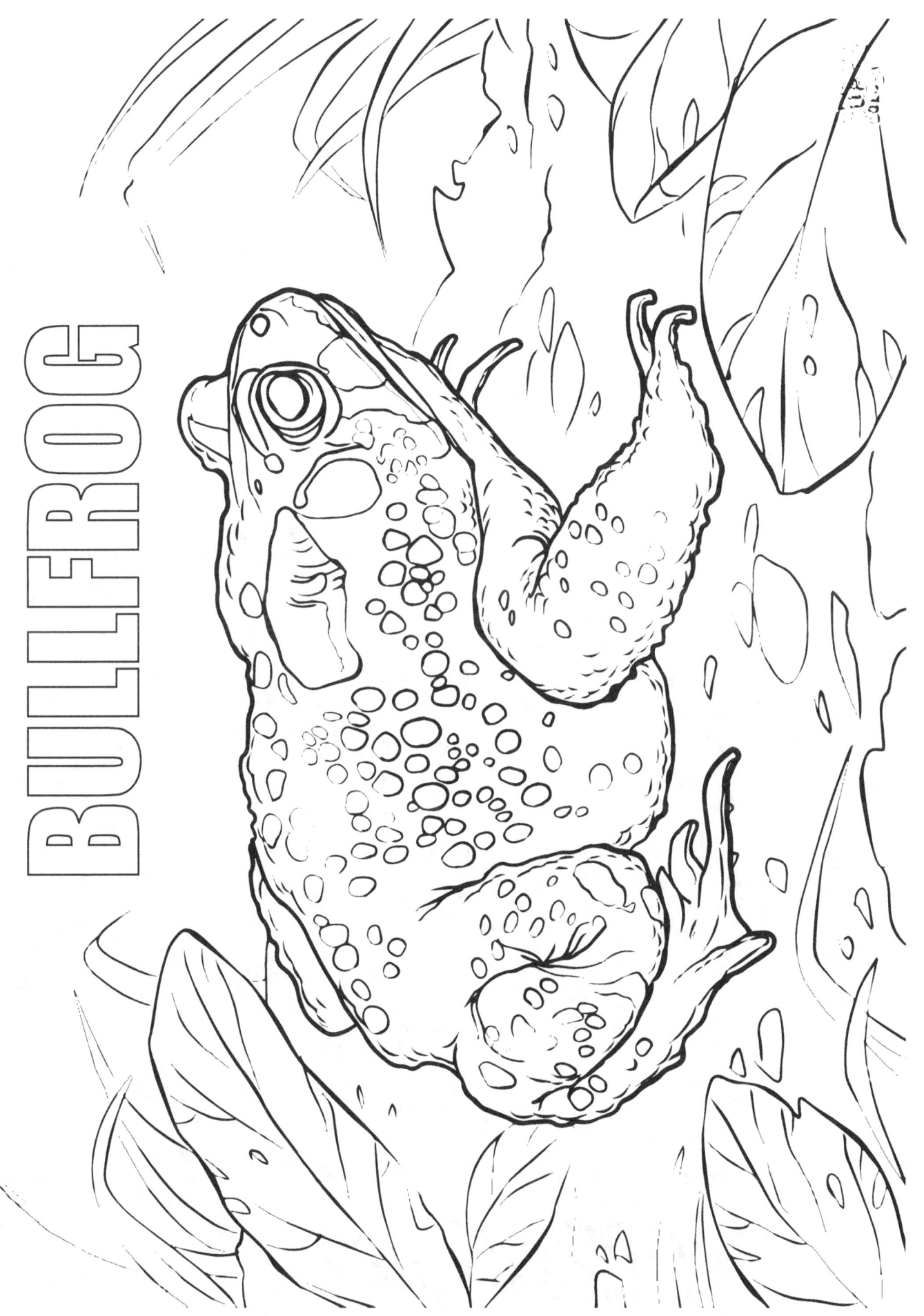

BULLFROG

Titi's Book

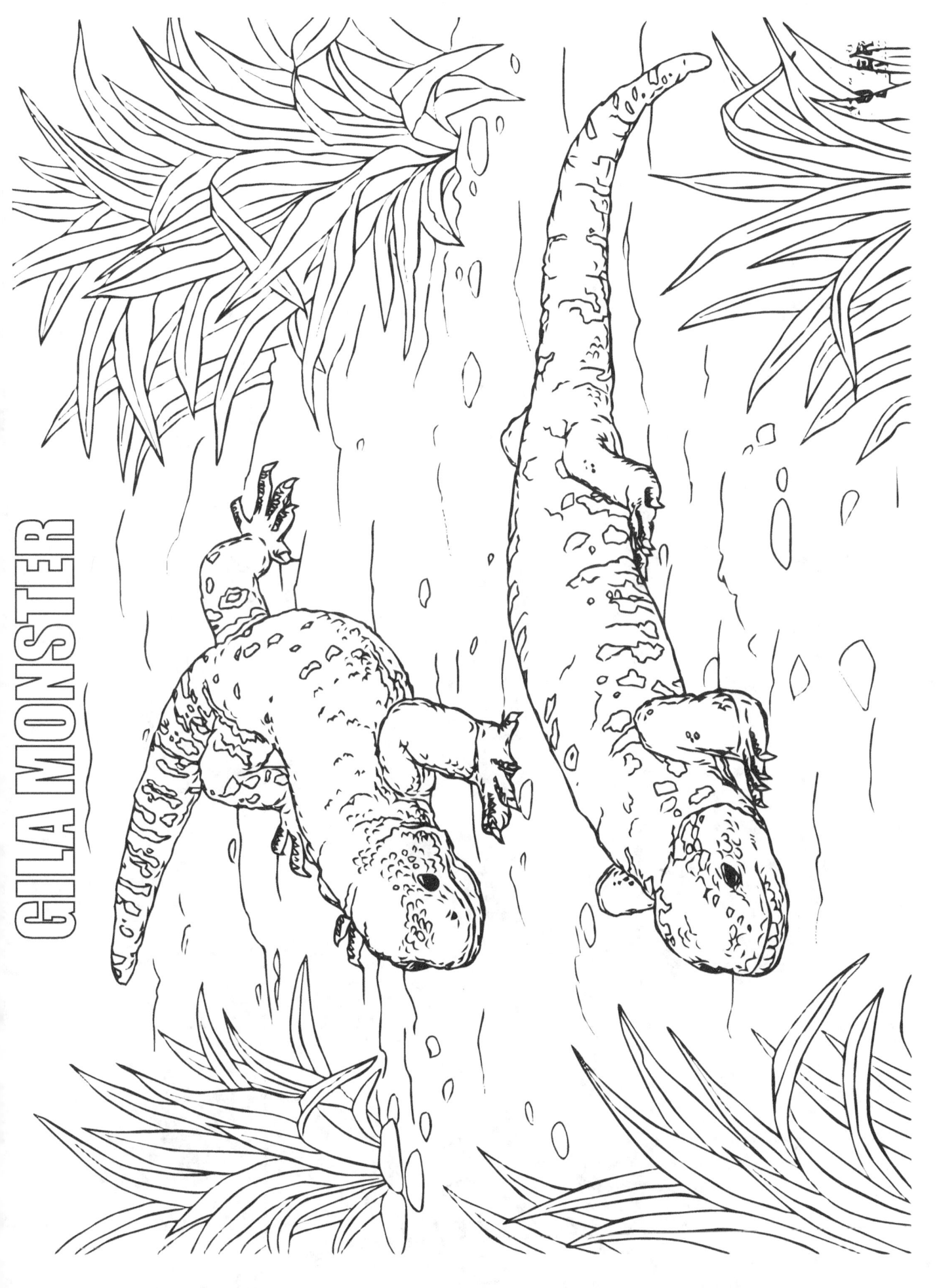

GILA MONSTER

Titi's Book

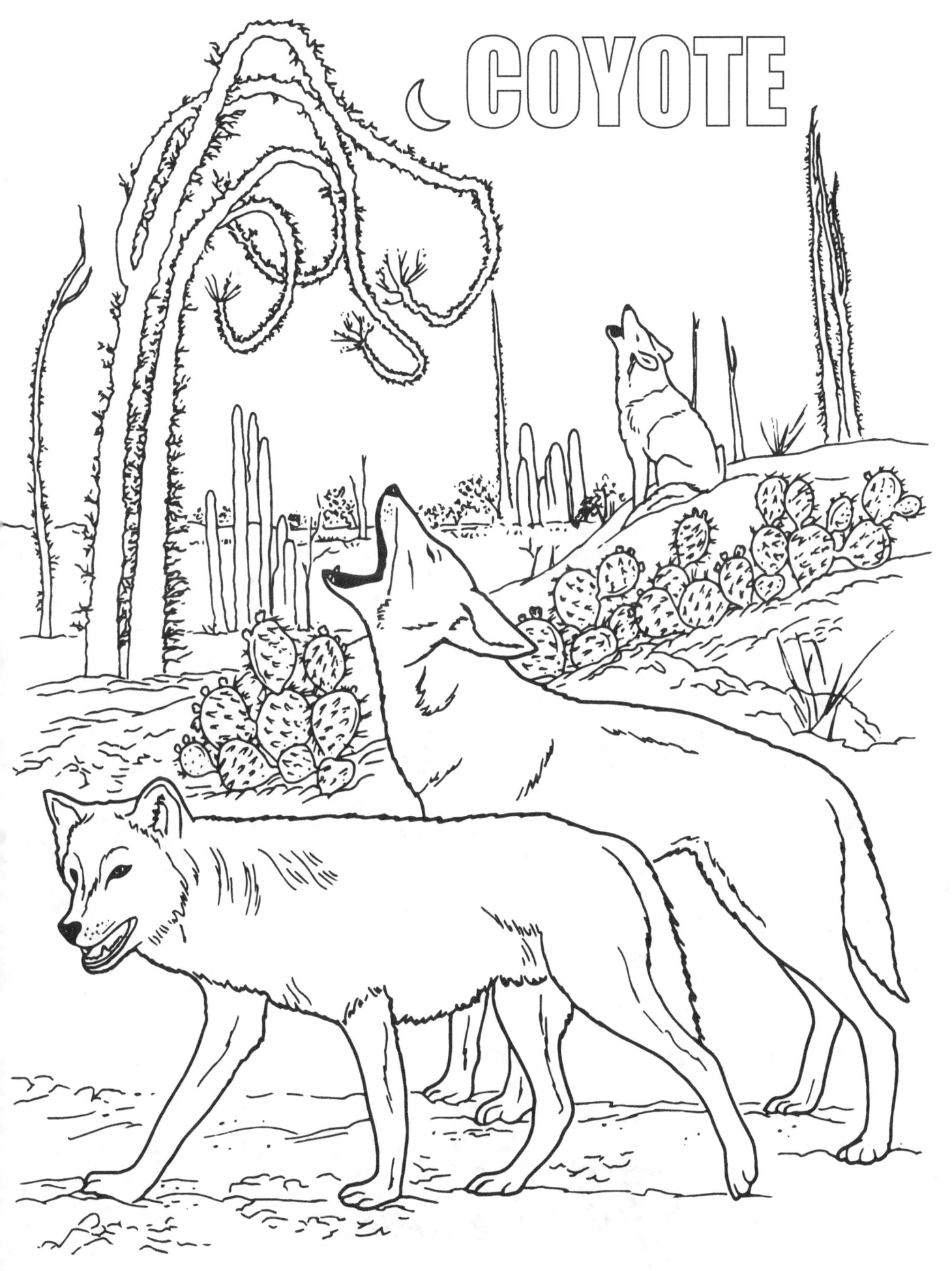

COYOTE

Titis Book

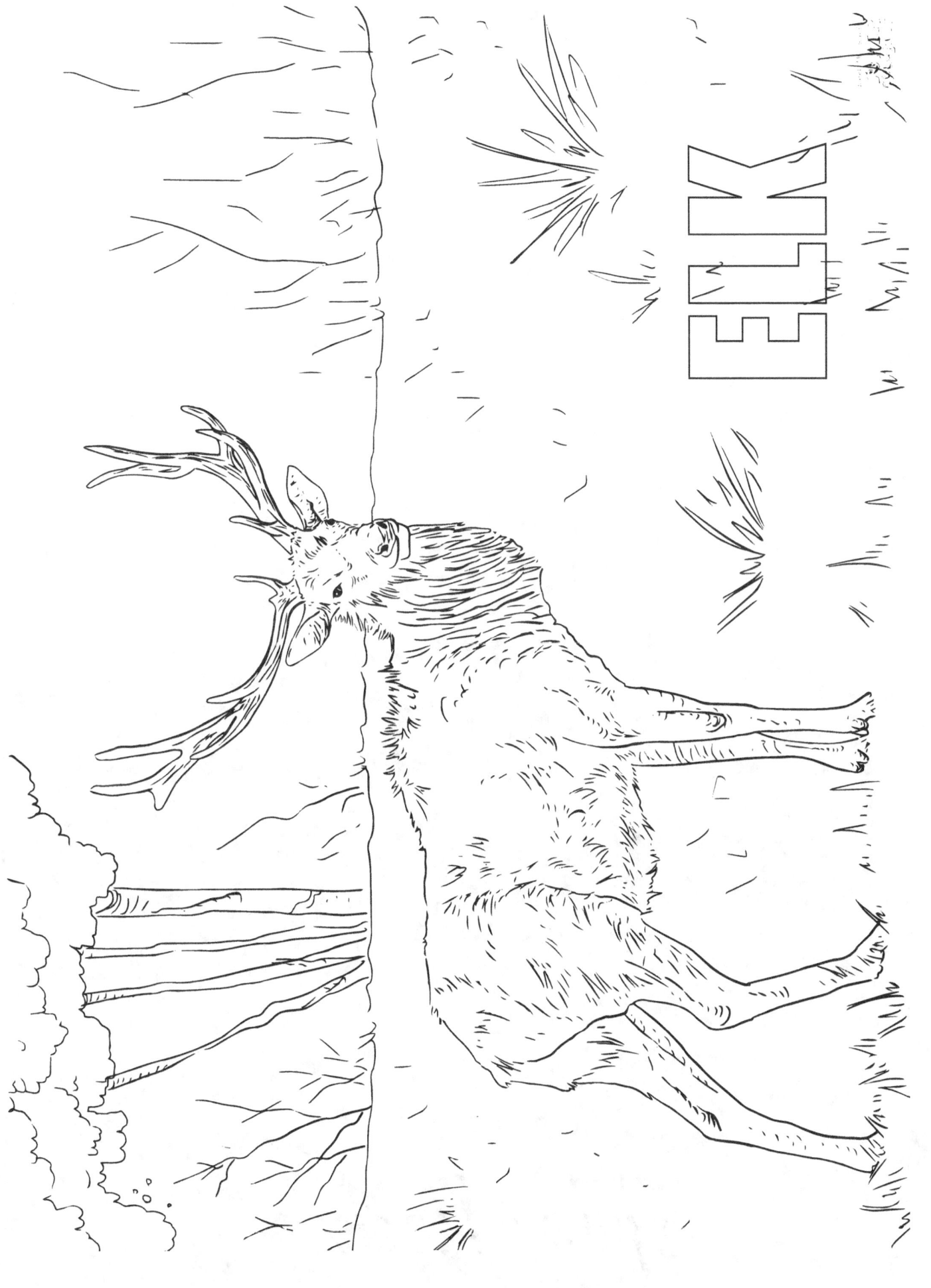

Titi's Book

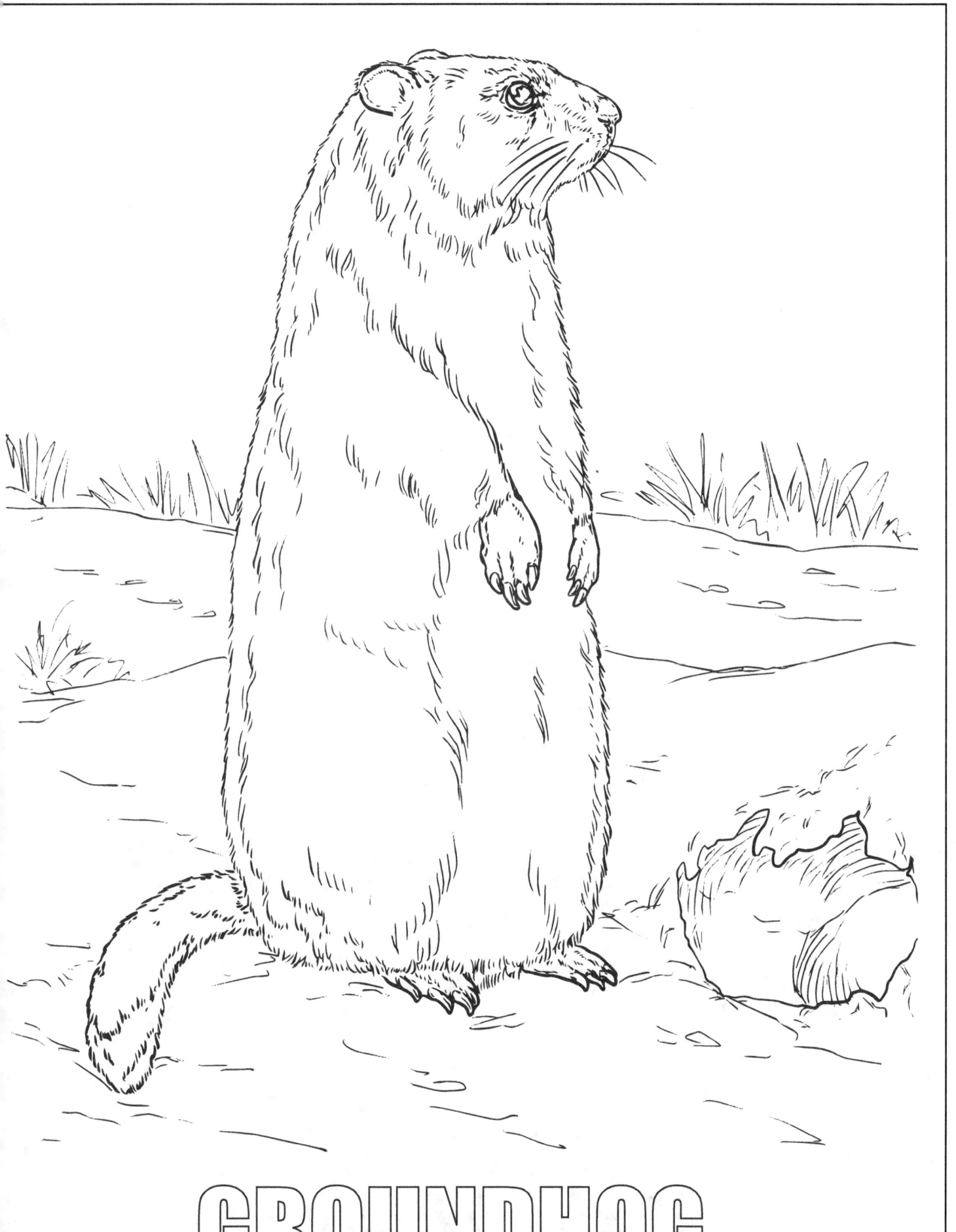

GROUNDHOG

Titi's Book

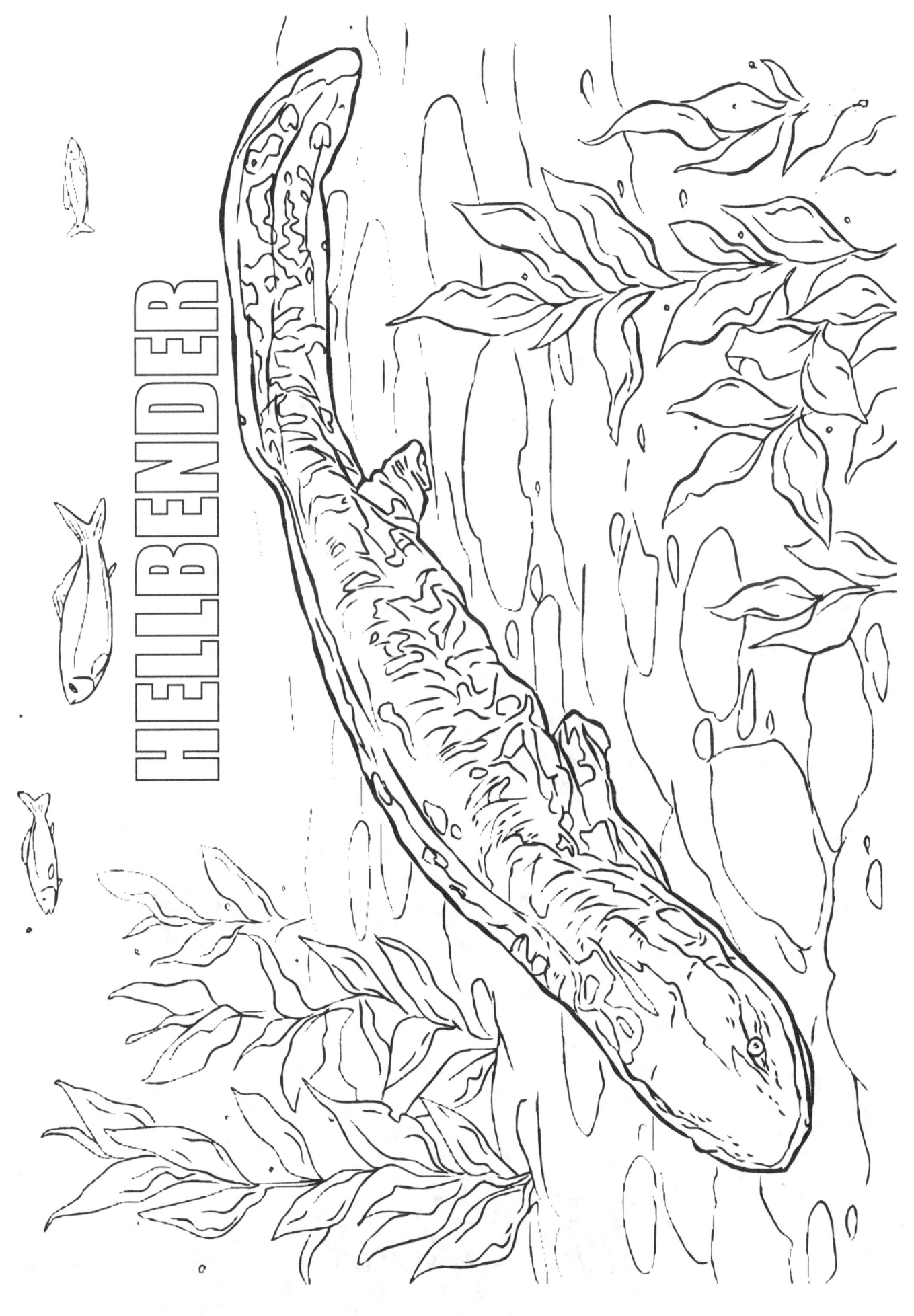

HELLBENDER

Titis Book

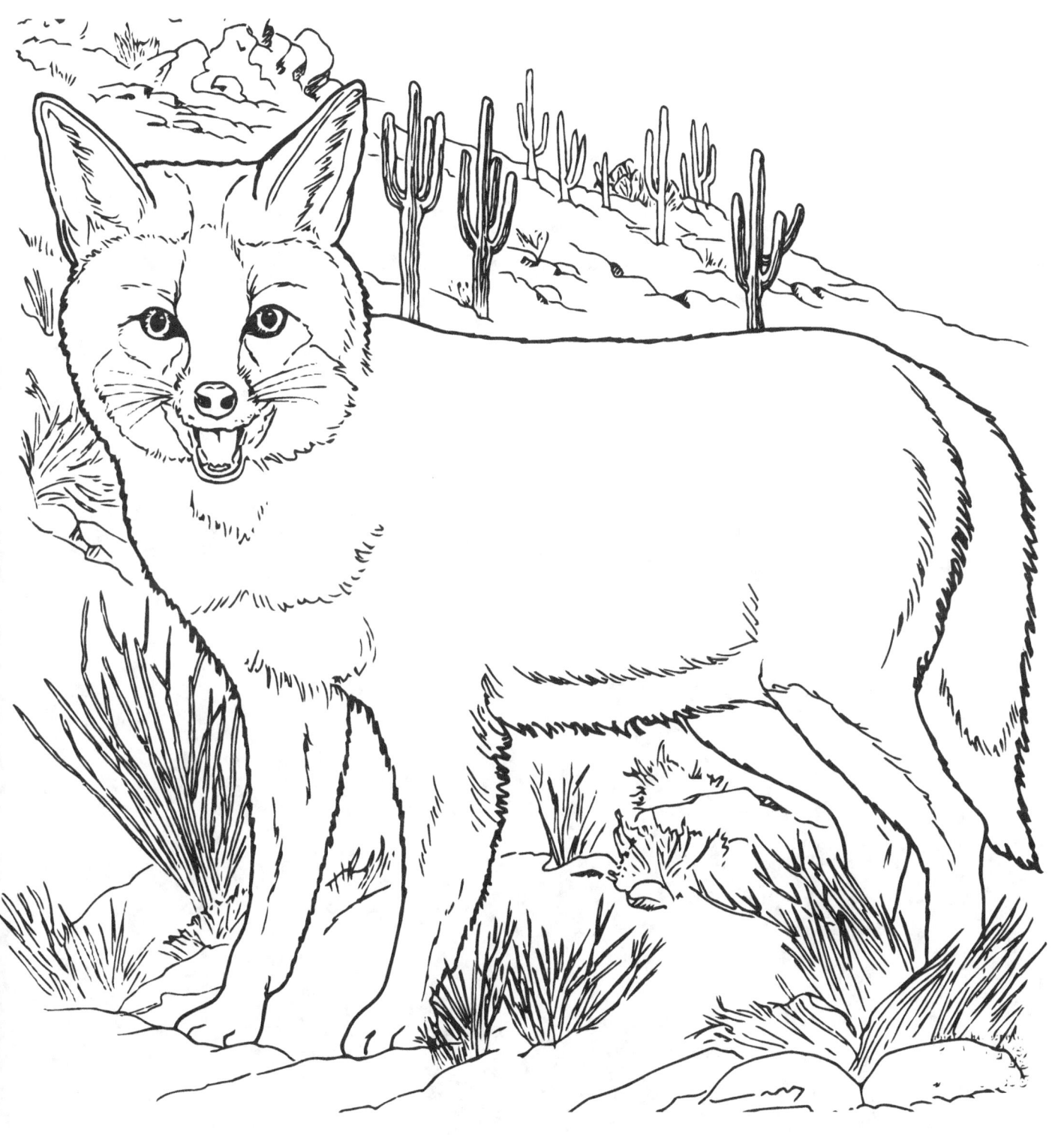

KIT FOX

Titis Book

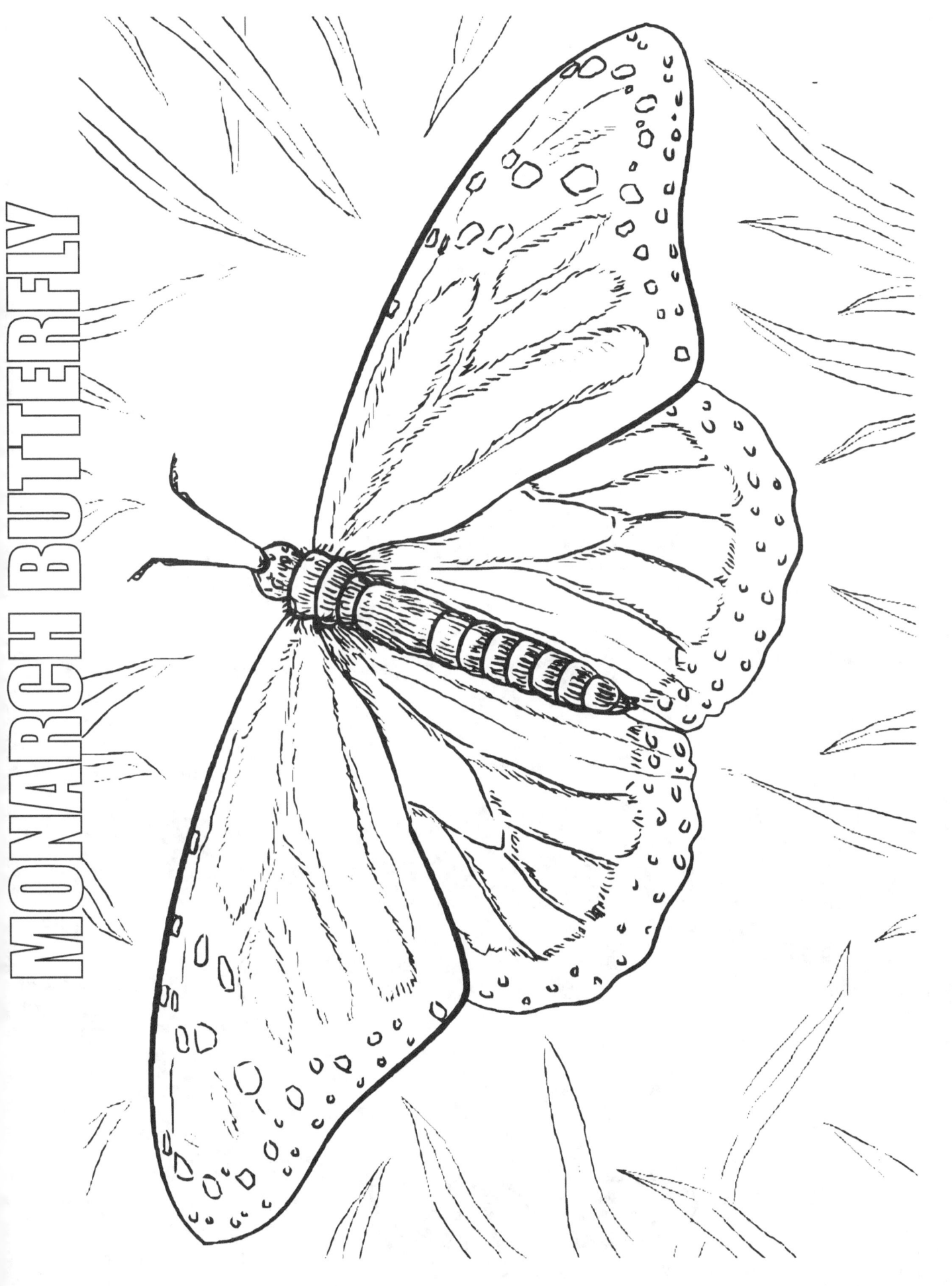

MONARCH BUTTERFLY

Titi's Book

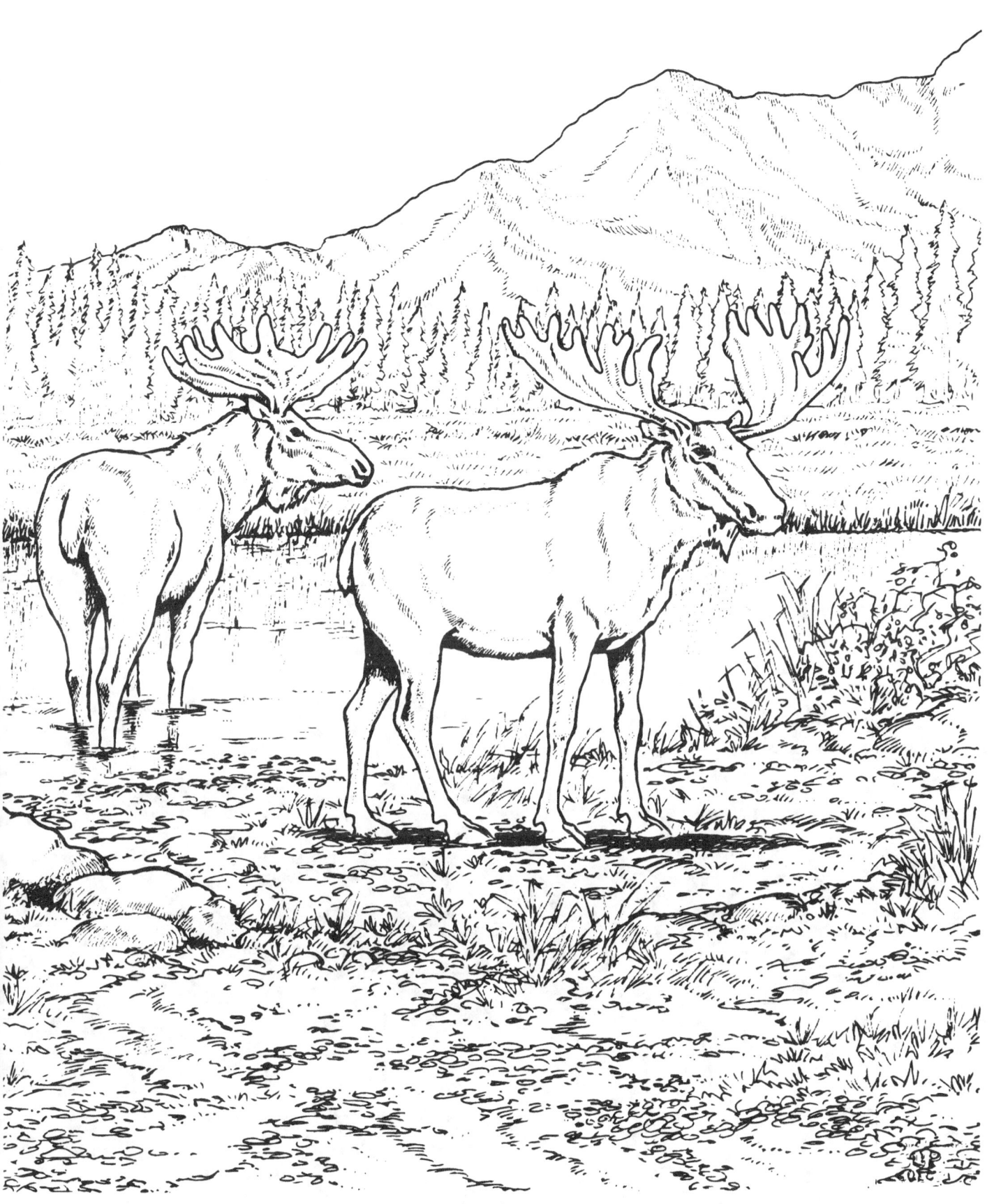

MOOSE

Titis Book

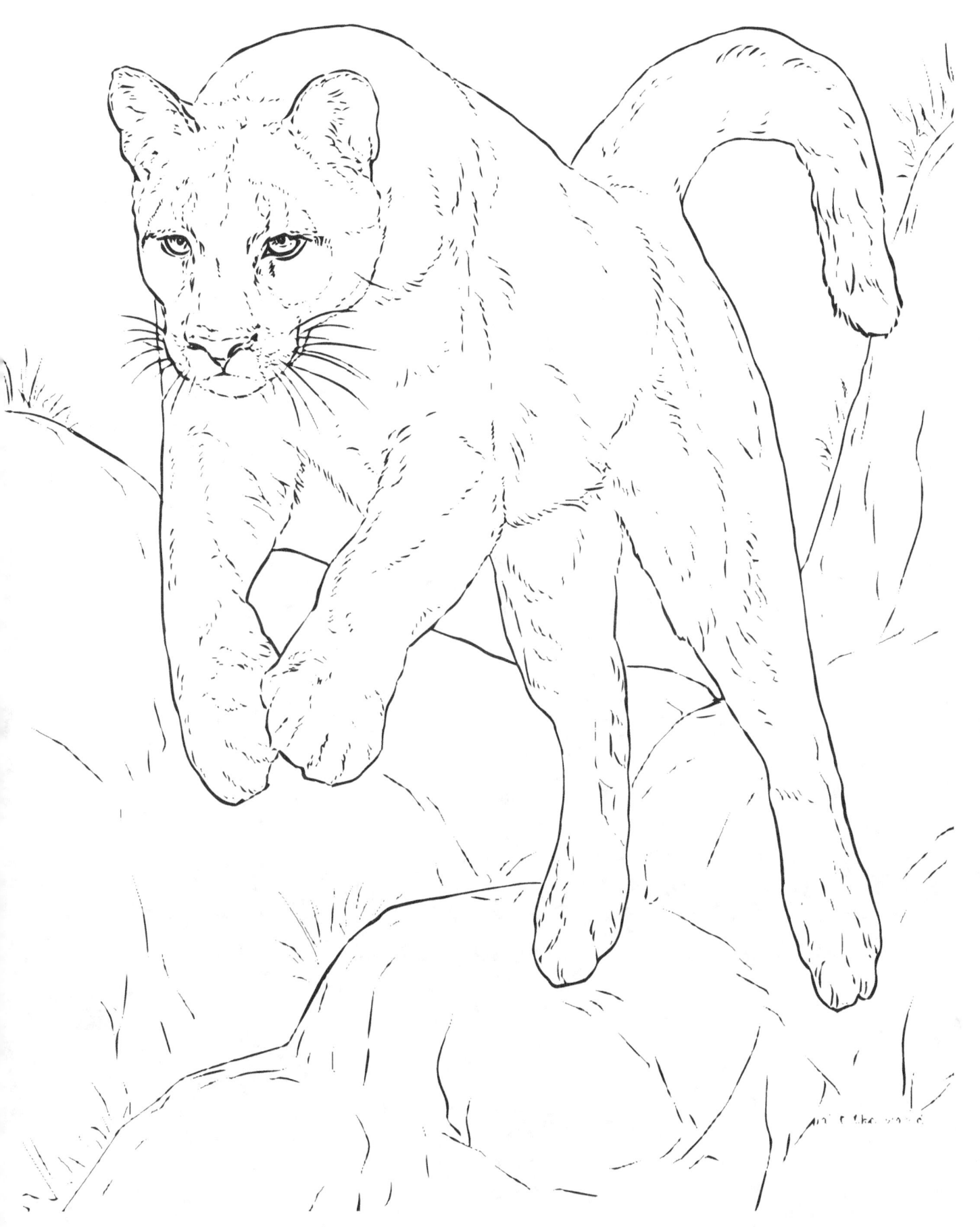

MOUNTAIN LION

Titi's Book

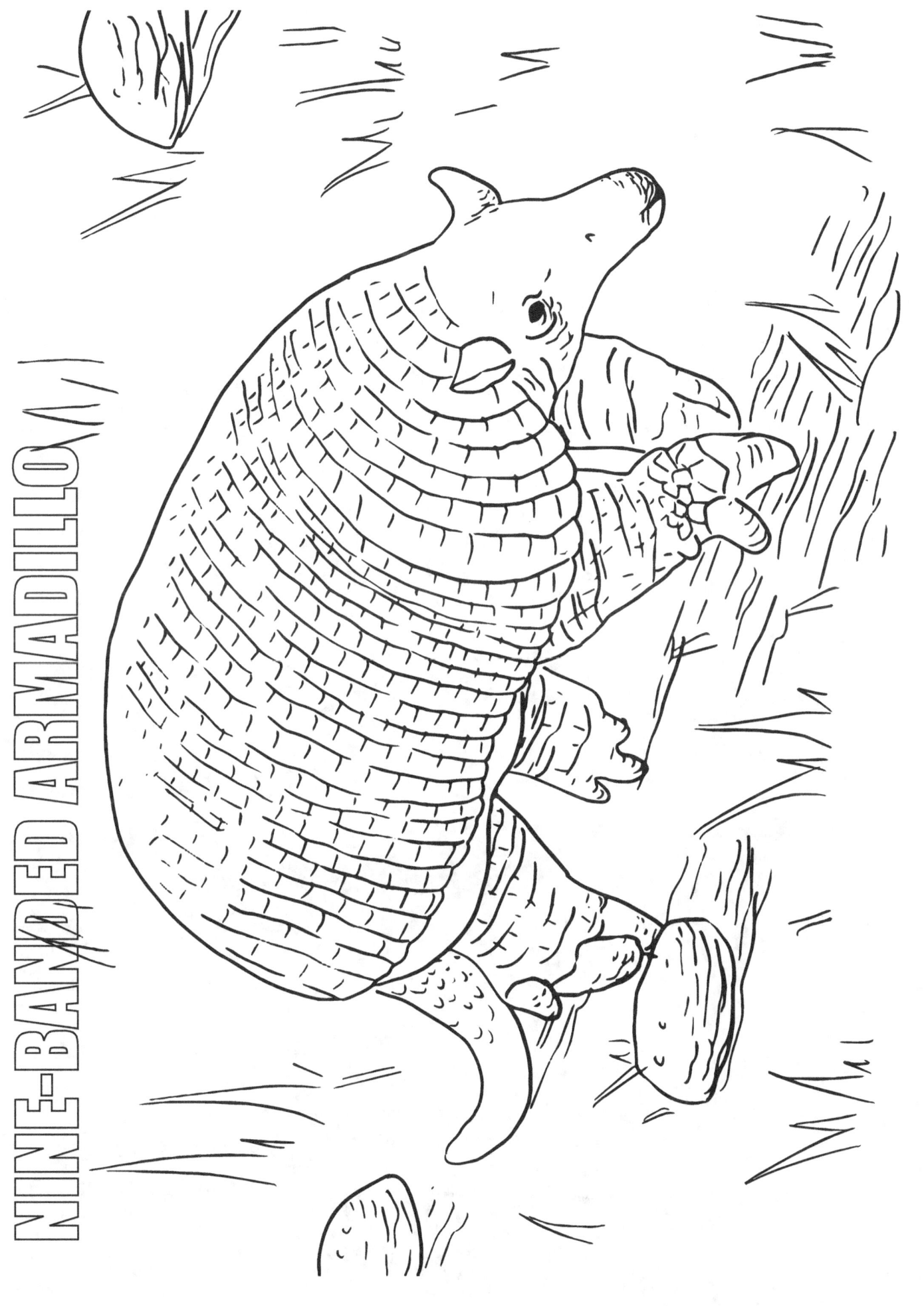

NINE-BANDED ARMADILLO

Titi's Book

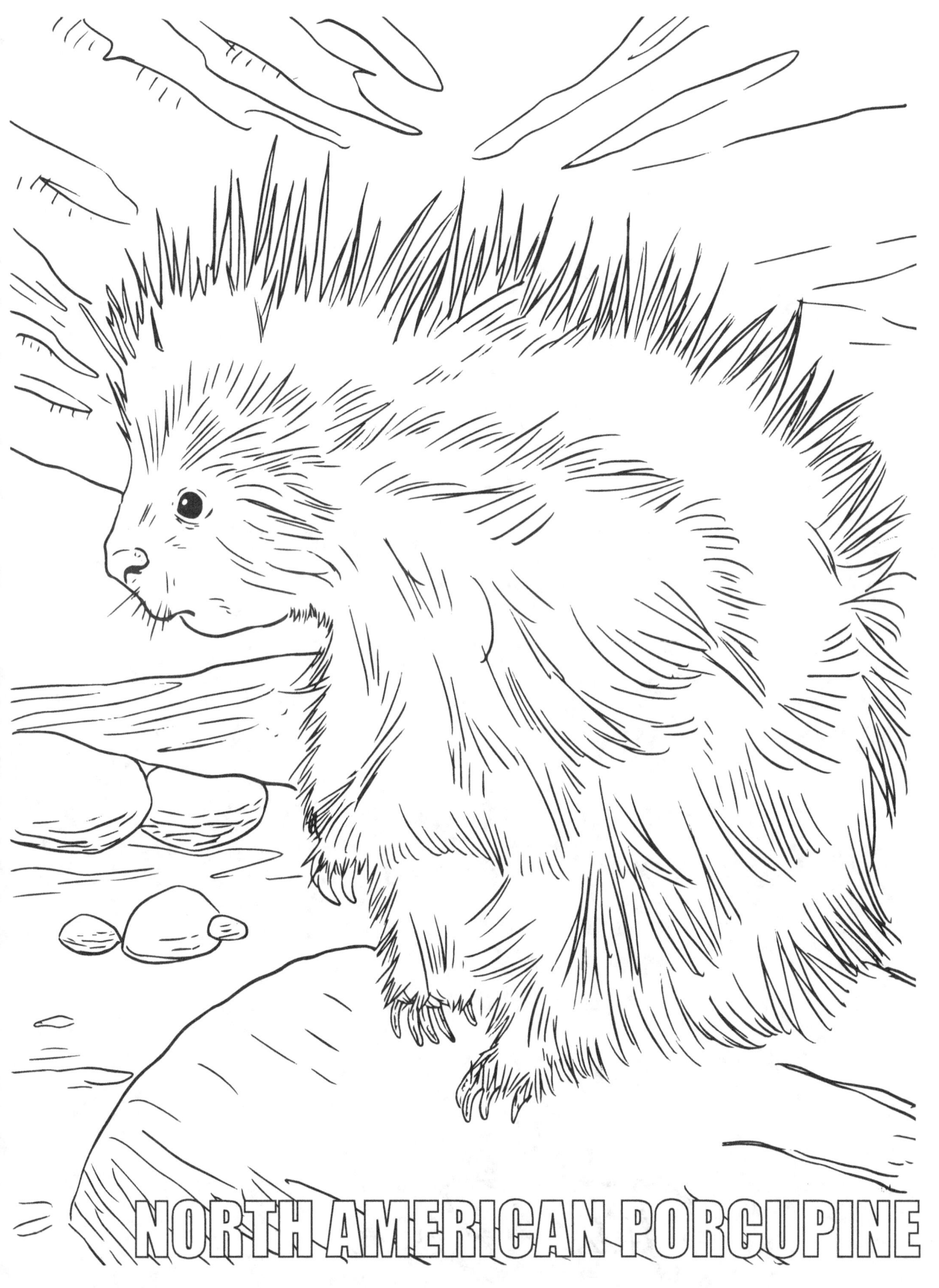

NORTH AMERICAN PORCUPINE

Titi's Book

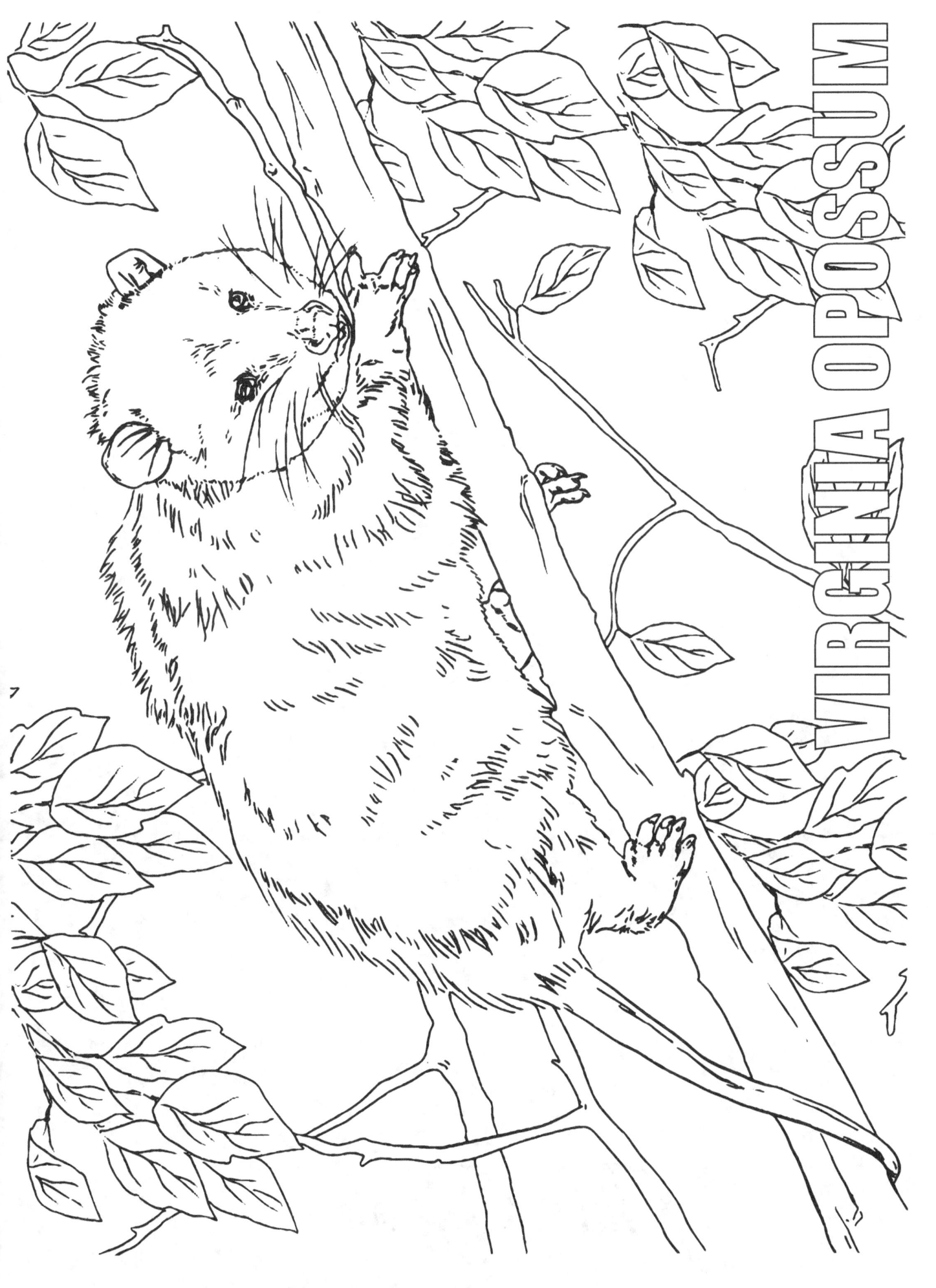

VIRGINIA OPOSSUM

Titi's Book

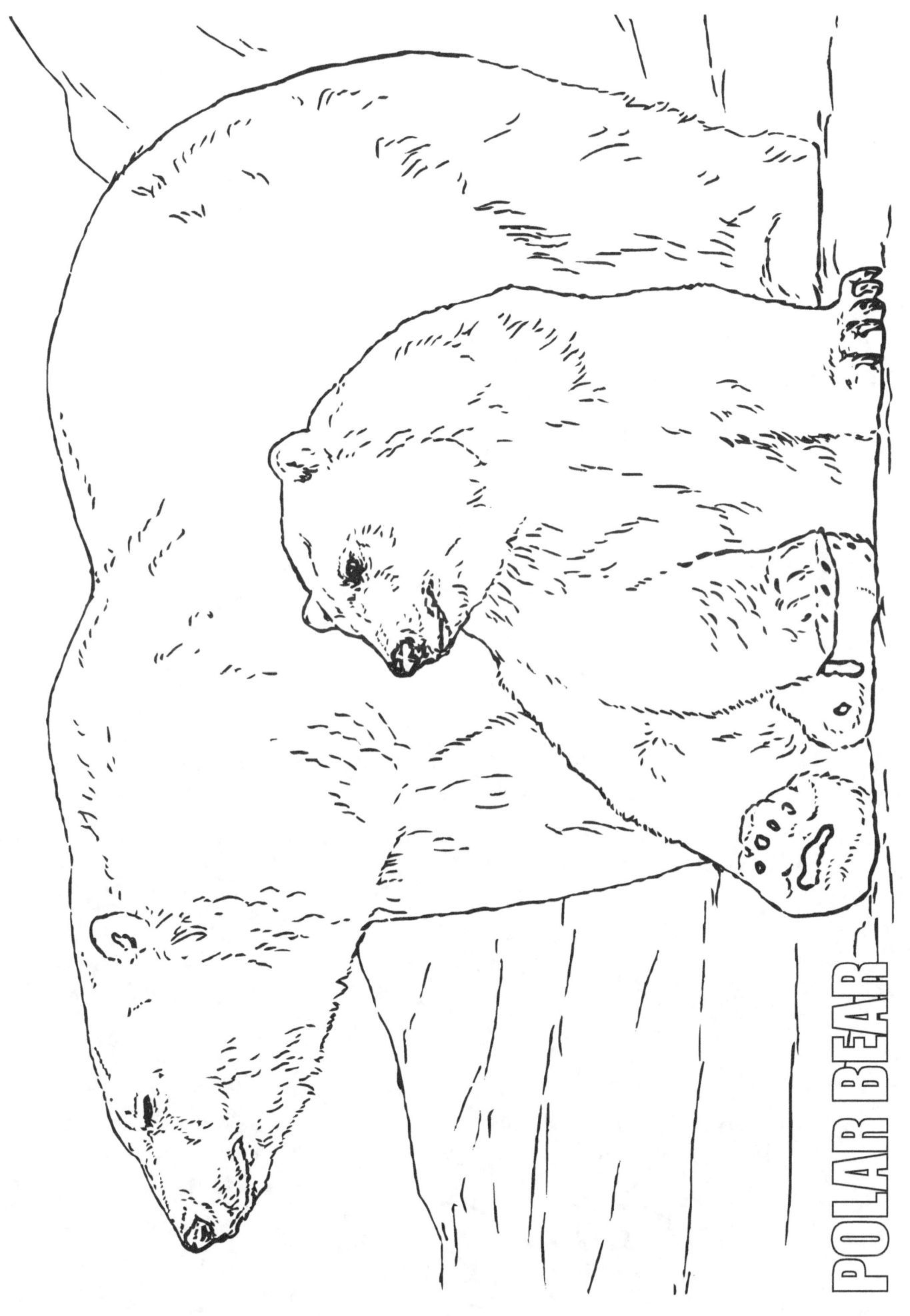

POLAR BEAR

Titis Book

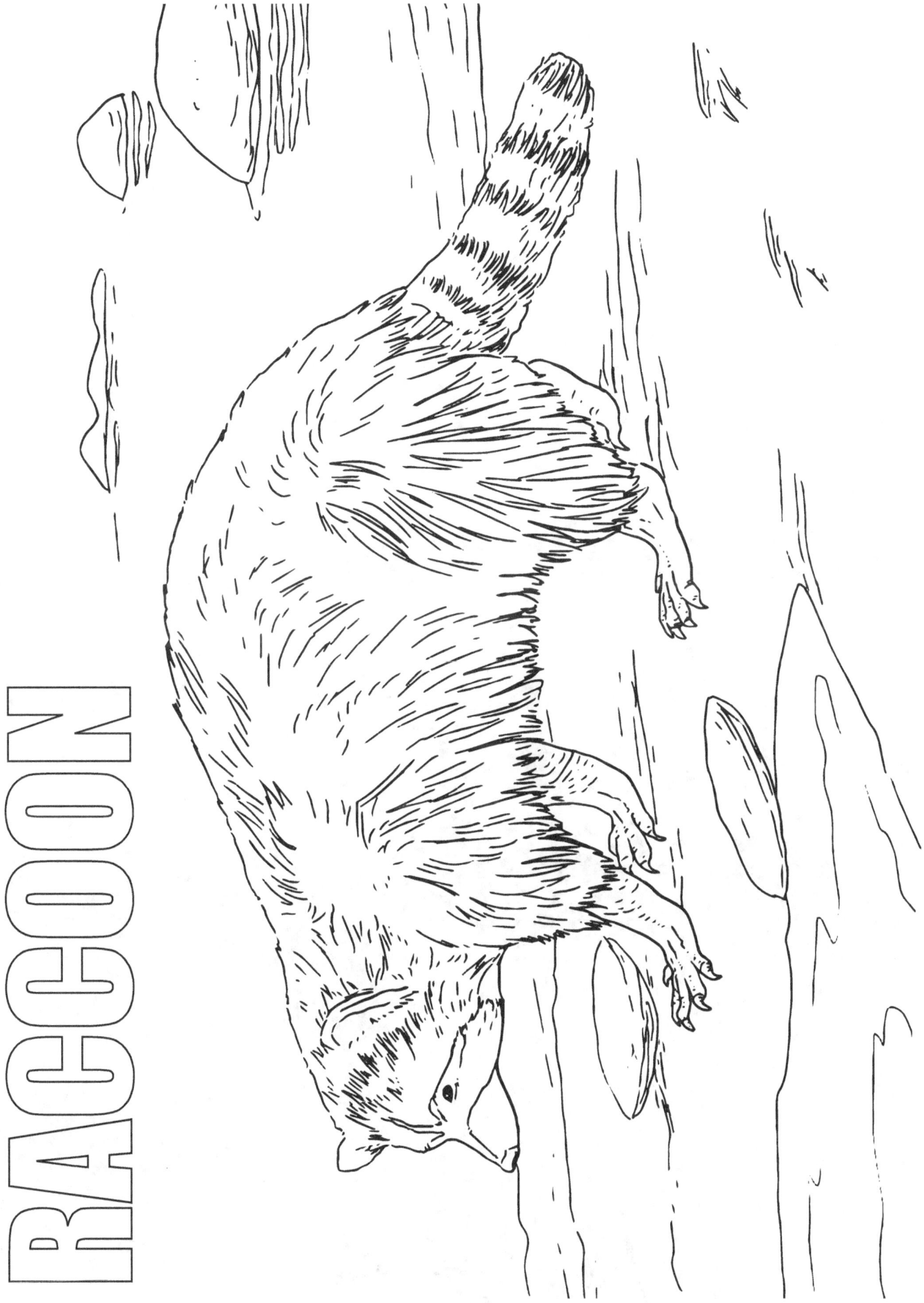

RACCOON

Titi's Book

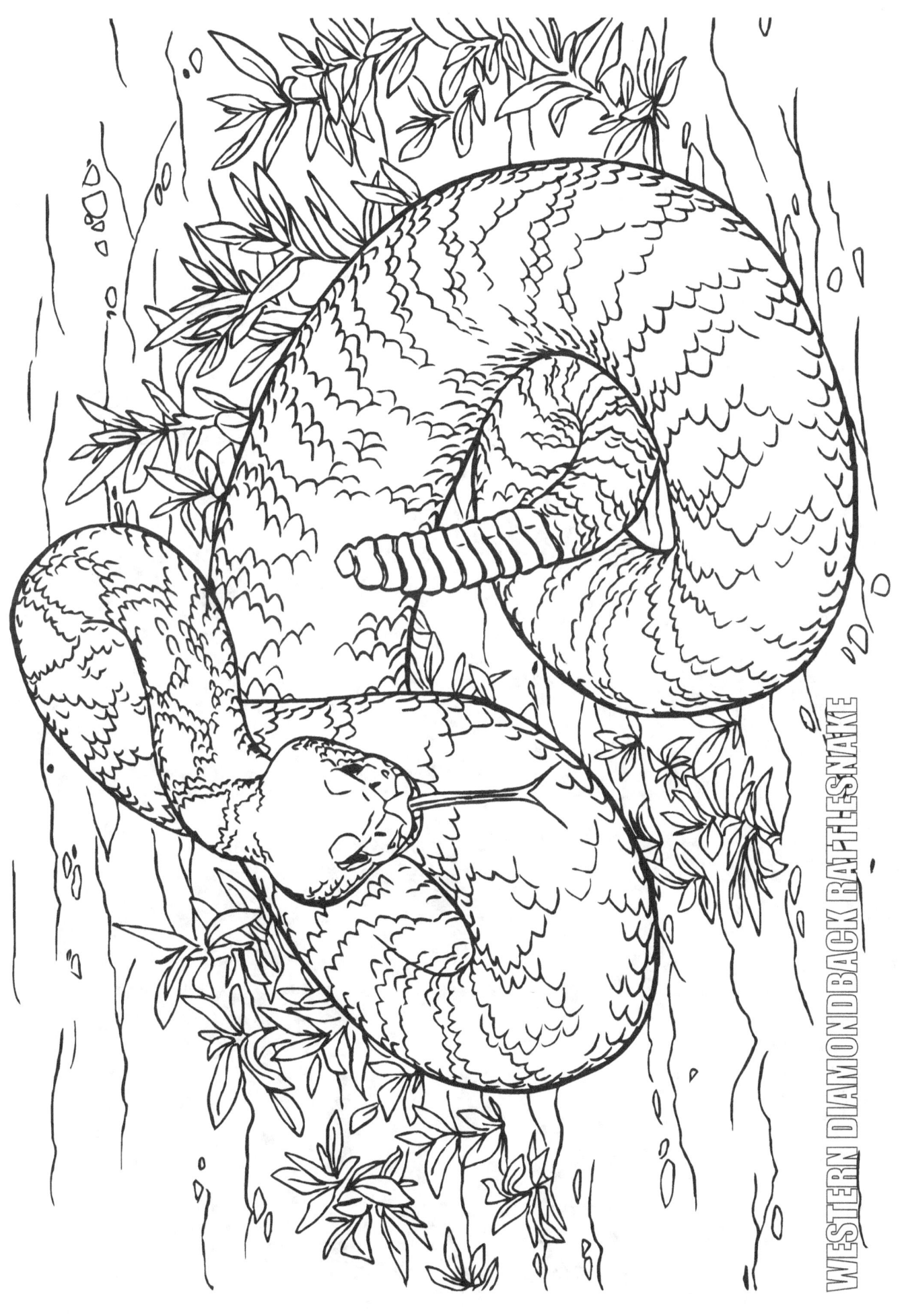

WESTERN DIAMONDBACK RATTLESNAKE

Titi's Book

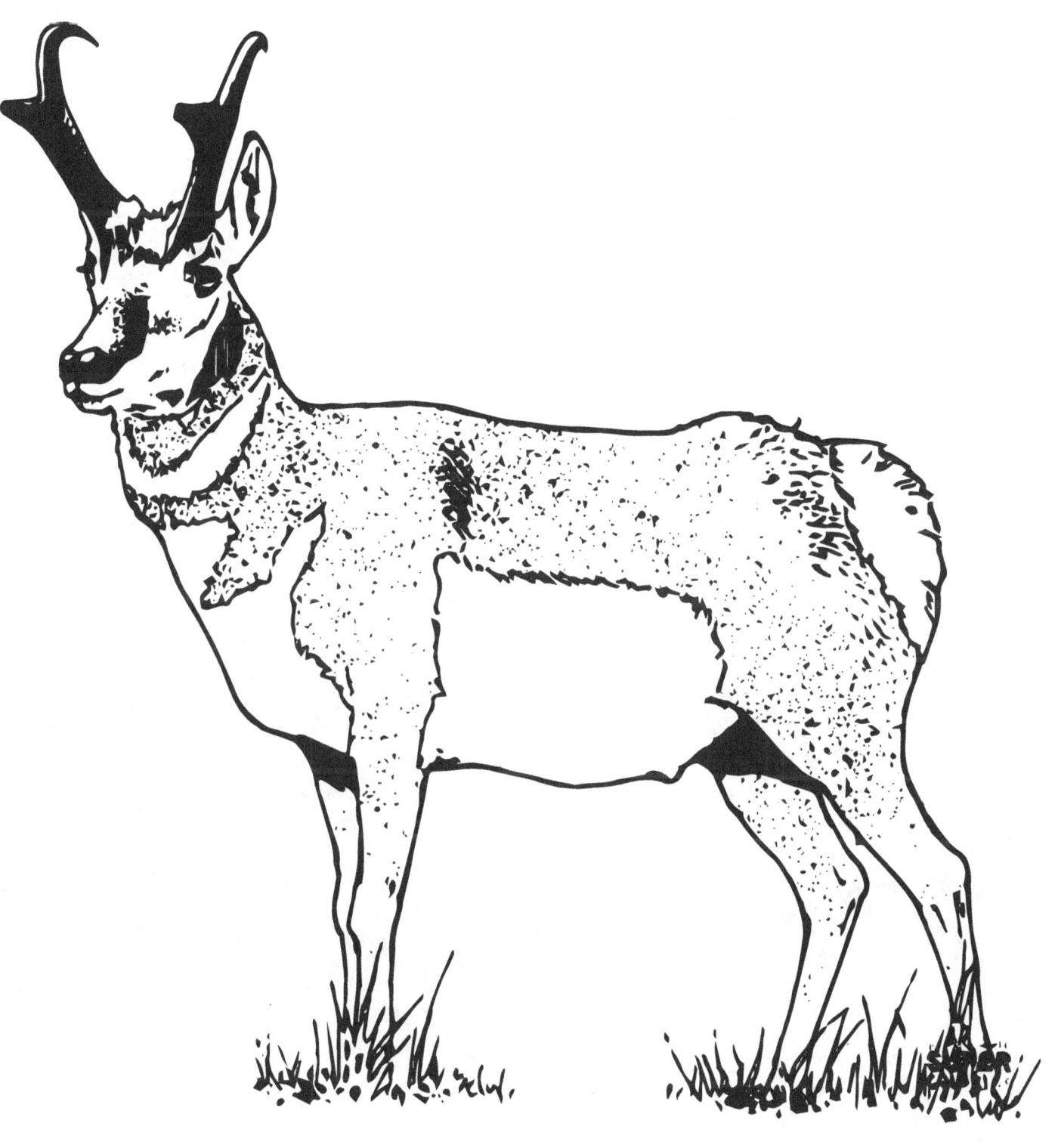

PRONGHORN

Titi's Book